Things That Make You Go Hmm...

A poetic tour of introspection and other curiosities

Christa A. Nuñez

iUniverse, Inc.
New York Bloomington

Things That Make You Go Hmm...
A poetic tour of introspection and other curiosities

iUniverse books may be ordered through booksellers or by contacting:

iUniverse
1663 Liberty Drive
Bloomington, IN 47403
www.iuniverse.com
1-800-Authors (1-800-288-4677)

Because of the dynamic nature of the Internet, any Web addresses or links contained in this book may have changed since publication and may no longer be valid. The views expressed in this work are solely those of the author and do not necessarily reflect the views of the publisher, and the publisher hereby disclaims any responsibility for them.

ISBN: 978-1-4401-5094-4 (sc)
ISBN: 978-1-4401-5095-1 (ebk)

Printed in the United States of America

iUniverse rev. date: 6/12/2009

Contents

rain and sun

it rained, seems like for years, one farmer said to another
beautiful big drops like the size of an owl's eye
fell one after another in succession, enough to water the crops with some
left over
the well was full for a spell, and we wasn't thirsty no time

it kept raining and, even after the wells was full, it rained s'more
seems like right after we thanked the Lord, we was beggin him for it to stop
it didn't stop, though, til it was good and ready and the water was ankle
deep in the shed and the children spent all day bailing it off the bedroom
floors

myrtle trees, tall an leafy, delivered shelter and we stood among them feeling
special, like they was ready-made umbrellas, like those ones in costa rica
called *sombrillas de pobres*. We sho' was poor, but we was dry for a while and
that felt good.

Pretty soon, the rain trickled off till it wasn't more than a spit of it on the
ground
All the land round the place turned green, green like you never seen before
And the hills were alive with crickets and birds, sound like a jungle, though
we was in California those days.

It didn't rain, and we was glad; needed a break, see.
We got the covers hauled off the stores to see what had kept and what got
ruint.
Seemed like we'd have ta start all over.
So we did. And it was good to work in the sun and not feel rain so, where
the color felt bout to wash right off ya.
The sun shone. We were surprised that it rose early and set late so early in
the season, but we lay down, in the light of a bright moon, near bout ever
night. We was happy.

The sun shone day after day, our sweat came early and ran through the day
clear into our shoes and wet the ground beneath our feet. It was the only
wet that poor ground felt in months. We wasn't so happy to provide it.
The sun beat and throttled us and that ground and the crops too. Those
stores were leaner than when the rot got 'em. We thot we was gon' die.

Sometimes we hoped for it, lookin up at that sun, strong as ever and gettn' stronger and we wished that long white whip would come out of the sky and kill us once and for all.

But it didn't. Pretty soon, it cooled off too. Skinny, burnt, tired and all, we survived. See this tea-stain on my hand? Won't never go way. I carry it like a badge of honor: The rain and sun whipped me long and hard, but they didn't whip me for good.

The farmer smiled a gummy smile and spat.

"Mmm hmm…" sighed the other farmer. "Been through that."

eye of the needle

I saw the Twin Towers Fall
I survived, but at a price.
I am bloody bones: the rich man, crushed in the eye of the needle
I am ripped through the needle that mends the tear, patches the hole in the
universal soul of humanity
It mends the tears, or rather dabs the tears that fall from woebegone, shut
eyes
I am a broken down thread, strung along wisdomless corridors of ignorance.
I experience yet another Dark Age. There have been more than one, for
sure.
I am strung along, in hope, I am sewn deeply into the fabric of a tired and
confused, yet titillated and stimulated America
I hurt, I pain, I'm worn out and worn again.

In times of war and division, a soldier, a housewife, a dog, a pretty green
lawn serve as a warning. Life is not as simple as this. Tomorrow is not
promised. Your son, your daughter, your neighbor, your friend, you
could lose them, you could lose them and not even notice that it not only
happened to you, it happened to a nation, a continent, a world.

Peace loving nations experience war, lose their proud young men: some
glory seekers, some avengers, some poor in search of a better life—some
aimed at the goal of going to college and make a decent living and pleasing
their families with minivans and 2.5 children; some aimed at pleasing the
God they've been taught and the opportunity to lay next to a million virgins
when the world is so dirty dirty dirty.
Many nations lose many of each kind of man.
We all weep. This loss, this hurt, this circle of grief, it happened to you and
me, to both heaven and earth; we share commonalities simple as swatting
houseflies, as complex as loving innocent children and elderly ladies.
the universe even saw and wept. Wept for you, for your loss, your greed,
your envy, your love and emptiness. The universe wept for you. the flow
mounted, tear for tear, pain for pain, love for love, more deeply than you
will ever know. It grew into a volcano of aged, flowing hot magma aimed
at the terrified village of a workaday public. We didn't even see it coming.
There's no getting out of the way. And when it hits, it strips, it cuts, like
that piece of glass that scraped my cheek when the towers fell. Burns, like
that woman, that gray ash-covered woman who walked up Park Ave. with

her briefcase covered in soot, refusing help, unable to do anything but shake her head in echoed negation.

When they fell, they left a hole, they left a hole in my heart. Death happened before my eyes. Death happened on a sunny day in September. The sun shone. It was a BEAUTIFUL day.

One of those days you lay in bed and watch the light shift, glimmering a shining advertisement of a new day across the ceiling of your Village apartment. You lie there and thank God, thank Him, for allowing you to see another day, to be able to sleep in. Sleep in, by God, the one blessing of temporary unemployment. And you revel in it until mid-morning, when a palpable hush falls over the neighborhood.

When you walk to that corner of Christopher and Broadway, there is a hole where you used to dance, used to twist and shake looking down out of the Windows of the World. They are shattered now, and no-one, no-one knows why or how.

That is the true meaning of terror. Being attacked and not knowing why or how. I know what that feels like, and I also know the guilt of being unharmed. The ridiculous feeling of safety and security amid chaos, the heart-soothing comfort of being singled out from those who left their bodies on the walk just blocks from my house, the knowledge that I have been watched and protected, on a day I had no right to be.

What I have was not easy. What I have was expensive; too rich for my blood. I was squeezed through the eye of a needle too narrow for my bourgeois sentiments and my lazy-minded concessions to my own sin, the death I flirt with, the life I hold on to at the last possible moment. I have never been able to forget the grace that brought me through. That grace belied the obesity of my soul, pulling me through the narrow door to the openness, the impossibility, the unexpectedness of forgiveness.

That grace left me dangling on a precipice of bitterness & prevented me from holding my hands over my ears and screaming for the truth to just shut up and leave well-enough alone. I want to scream it even if there is no "well-enough". "Well-enough" never existed and I know that. Still, the

4

ocean of tears sends breakers of stillness over my heart. I have been saved, when I shouldn't have been.

As those in a church boasted, "Not one of us was harmed. Not a single hair of our heads nor any of our family members." And I smiled and felt chosen. It wasn't until now that I learned to scream. HOW DARE YOU!! HOW DARE YOU!! Jesus himself left his blood on the walk. Why not you? Why not me? Why not all? I scream and I still live, I still eat hamburgers, drink tea, poop every morning. Where would I be now if I had left my flesh, my blood on the pavement? Faith does fly under the burden of such questions. But it always comes back. Whether I answer correctly or not, it returns to me, a familiar and friendly face. It winks at me, knowingly. I cast my arm round its sweet shoulders.

Death has come within earshot, we did not exchange words. I received just a nod from Death as I gazed wide-eyed; half-conscious of my stance behind the kind of thick glass one is grateful for at the zoo. This day, death has claimed and fed on human souls, parents and children, even cats, dogs. My soul is unconsolable. Death hangs around, gorging itself repeatedly, the years hence. Delicacies: the death of hope, death of logic, death of promising futures, death of planned success, death of possibility, death of romance, death of relationships, death of innocence, death of trust, death of the promise life seems to hold, the promise that seems, oh it SEEMS, unending to the young and untried. As I inhale the black smoke that pours daily from downtown and hangs over the Manhattan skyline for months, the threat of cancer is whispered from the other side of the glass. The glass is not thick enough keep that away. I feel this threat, and it chills me to my bones.

Violence has it's day today. Adds it to a few more days, weeks, years, millennia just to be sure of its supremacy. It had it's day today, it would have its day tomorrow if it could claim what is left unpromised to us all. Yet, my human mind believes violence will reign tomorrow too. I am not proven wrong. I watch violence as if behind thick glass, where it is I who pace, who stalk the ethereal smoke and mirrors that has captivated the nations. Violence pretends to march methodically, act strategically when, in reality, it doesn't think, doesn't care, is never satisfied, never succeeds quite enough. It is the one thing beneath which the earth trembles, one thing that will not say "Enough!" Violence, and its expert shedding of innocent blood, has its day. Violence saddens me from afar and would not scare me if it were closer. Violence is afraid of love and those who wield it. Bestial violence has its day, but not that coming precious hour. Doom, once its friend, will be the black hole that swallows and separates it from all the children, all the friends, all the loved neighbors and innocent pals who dangle from its maw.

I try not to let hate drown me. I drown all the same, some that drown next to me have the ability to laugh even when there is no air. I try to learn this trick and choke. When I feel like all is about to burst, bloody taste in my mouth, I am pulled through…the eye of that needle, I pass and pass, impossibly yet assuredly, through the narrowest of passages. I fall out on the other side, weeping, soul-bare, bereft and gasping for air on the bank of that bleak undertoe of this lost, lost, stupid, sad world.

Pulled through the eye of the needle, my spiritual deadness died that day. Amid imminent death, evident and seemingly victorious death, I came alive. For the first time, I see clearly that life is worth living. I stepped into fresh and expectant, in triumph.

A Psalm

Above ancient waters, formless darkness and mist.
Separated smoky corridors, and heaven from Abyss.
Then Creation yawned newborn, dew-laden and sweet-scented.
First breaths just taken, a Father contented.
Diligent love was best and never bested.

...

Brilliant patience wins hearts through peaceful ferocity.
Blessings appearing whilst asleep. Echoes of prosperity.
Compassion new-arising, daily for a people fallen.
Lame spirit bound in warmth forever woolen.
Promises kept – nourishment as sweet as stolen.

...

Laws to remember, they seem to forget.
Forgiveness pierces hearts, deadly as a bayonet.
Consciences seared, peeled new and pricked sharply.
Awaken fast to inner decay formed grossly.
Dismay, redemption, sure death escaped only narrowly.

...

Drawing from the deepest well, we return.
See time end with a Phoenix's burn.
Arise as transitory epochs ebb gladly away.
Look at hands, once made from clay.
Emblazoned and changed on that great day.

Don't Kill Me, I'm an Artist

Like women in stilettos, we absorb the highly configured fantasies of the post-modern man.

We say the N word. Let it slide off our tongues in brotherhood and in contempt. Contemptible brotherhood mediums our slang.
Cold languages warmed by alley cats.
Original man slinging avant garde-ism like it's centuries old, because it is.
We say the N word like it's a soul clap. We propagate to ever changing times, the quick scratch always itching our palms, buying ivory and turning it black.

Is it a shame? Such a waste, right? Flirting with disaster, edge-dwelling man wasting dough on a bagel. Spiced with the salt of the Earth, which makes it sweeter. We live on the echoes of a thunder clap, tune in interpretive eyes to life's lightning in the distance.

Calling it the hustle, weaving scams' skeins into kinte cloth and burning it at a noticed moment because a treasure is worth nothing if not a sell.

So true when you haven't the time to tell.

Who does? …When the city is hot and the pimp is cold. And Johnny skyrockets on a Blood's voided soul. Gotta be quick on the draw.
…

Running first, last to get the –ward (since there ain't no re-)
Snatch your guts and they bleed all over. Blood runs forever, marking time as a bum drinks wine. Never stop.

Trip the light a thousand times and still come up in darkness.
Human balm on the wound of ages. Sopping up the sticky salve of consumerism with a raw tongue.
Blister in the sun, sweating welter weights contending the winner in a set up.
Swinging mitts against the teats of Madame Battle Royale.
They're as big as Fort Knox and twice as tough. She lives there. Take off your mitts to mop the floor.

Our sweat never dries on the solid gold staircases. Hallowed hallways reek with the sweat of our fear and labor.
We smell only the green. Crisp.
Damp custodians whisper soft, the winners' names. Dropping their own in the rubble they sweep into the light at tunnel's end.
We'd never know when it was mislaid, and say we were misled.
Blaming the brown brother not yet across the river. His father and twin, hustling in time to the music in our souls.
We hear it. Say the DJ saved your life. Which life? The words and beats are synaptic shoot outs on the star count of a convict doing life and living death.
…

He sees the sun from a cell's cracked mirror and dreams of his freedom in my face.
I pose poetic in the nightmare of the leaders, whoever took it.
Each mops his own brow with the fact:
Affirmative Action is not retroactive.
Doesn't know we've done without it since the first action was just a thought.
Seals their doom with that bit of ignorance.
And we rejoice, dance a carnival in our hearts and plan…
I'd call that a pipe-dream if I smoked.

Africa

Bloody sea between
Golden waves of wheat
And sunny vale over diamond mines
To which do I belong?
So obscure does Africa sprawl
From coast gold or ivory, among trees or sand
I know not from which land I come
This blood so mixed in me
Blood of Europe, blood of Asia, blood of America, blood of our mother
Africa
I am the lost cousin of all, belonging wholly to none and partially to all
The continent calls me from across seas deep and wide
So strong is her call
I'd swim it, spiting current, shark, whales and all
So blurred, though, is my connection to her and all others as well,
I'd probably swim not north or south but simply away
Paddling brown, red, yellow skin tone
To the moon, forever to stay
...
So, is it to Africa I'll roam?
When it's to nowhere that I belong
Who can truthfully say where I'll sing my heart's song?
Surely not skin or ancestors
When the past and present circumstance spans the world from couscous to
High Tea
Yet, I've only heard of Farnsworth and Frederickson
I'm multicultural, and hail from the many coasts of nearly all the seas
Yet no-one can recognize me, truthfully.
My face is a wind-scattered song,
A puzzle undiscoverably destined as mine to belong
A song not heard for ages long gone
Yet, this is the one I'll marshall to greet the Dawn
...
And so if heaven smiles
Who am I to frown?
I say goodbye to ancestral sorrows
They are too numerous to tell
I move on, dutifully,

Carrying only my penny's ransom,
Cast into life's wishing well
…
Away, away…
Toothbrush, a hat and the clothes on my back
Sole effects that burden my track.
Say goodbye, with a wink and a sigh
Gloriously, finally, me, myself and I

guns and fish

guns and fish
both make their way to a Tanzanian airport
landing on an airstrip manned by crooks or drugged men,
men who sleep, deadened of conscience and mind

while some men sleep, other men from faraway lands
step onto airstrips where they command the owners of what lies under the
airstrip
to unload the cargo which will kill or maim their children in future times

once done, they load fish raped from waters, once again, not their own
and take it back to their homeland, faraway from the nightmare of Africa.

Mwanza, a strip of death, the point of entry for all the disease, all the death,
all the killing, the maiming, the raping of generation upon generation of
people without a hope or a plan.

Guns and fish mingle onboard a cargo plan. Guns for fish, as a country's
children starve, and, those strong enough to carry a rifle, march, heavily
armed, out into the misty hills to do to their future what has been done to
their past and present.

Starve because there are no fish
Kill because they have only guns and bullets to fill their bellies
Maim because their land lies crippled and crumbling beneath their feet
Destroy because their Mother-land is dying

Vicious hound

Here, gimme your money. Lay it on me and stand back. Watch 'em tear and listen to 'em howl. That one's screamin' like a baby ain't he? Pay up, it's over. Take that weak one to the pool. He ain't fit to live. Couldn't hold his own. That your boy, a little young ain't he. Naw, not too young to get a taste. You want a taste, boy. Pick your dog and watch him lock on, looka that grip. Ain't nothin' comin' outta there. That the death grip if I ever saw it. Don't cry now, boy, don'tcha cry. Ain't nothin' but some blood. why'nt you clean that up. Got another fight comin' up here. Wipe them tears, here they come. Set em up, that's right. That one look hungry. Like he could tear a hole in a car door. That's what I call a dog, a true dog, ready to kill, ready to kill today, any day, long's he gets a taste of another dog's blood. There goes the ear, hangin' on by a thread, should we call it? Let it go for another minute and see what happens. Never can tell. Seen some come back after losing an eye, a jowl. Everybody love an underdog. Yessir! Nope, that one's a goner. Hard when they so tired and chewed up can't even stand up for theyself. Get him out. May's well shock him to death, won't feel it no-how. Who's next? Who's got a fighter? I seen some vicious hounds in my day. That's a fact, and I ain't ashamed. This here is real life, boy, drink it up. I see he ain't lookin away no mo, huh Pop? He gon' be a fine boy. Set 'em up, whoo hoo!, they look hungry!

That one there had a fight last week. Killed the other one in less than an hour, they say. Came from a litter of that great bitch who fought and killed two in a night.

The boy goes home and remembers a dog, his pet, that bled out and died. He remembers the fight, the fight where no dog wins. They are maimed, their blood let til there is no more, as the minutes tick on, victory is further than ever.

Earmuffs in Southern California

Running backward down a one-way street
Keeping time with your rebellious gait
Clipping rosebuds with my feet
And stuttering my name
I looked at you and saw no more
As the last dance toasted in the first
You cried into a lonely telecast
So I wished to make a lip print on our shared champagne glass
Drunken promises to call fell into silence when you were gone
Striped shirts still in my washer
They smell like Dawn at dusk
Rainy mornings in bed with the lights off and no food in the fridge
You order my breakfast as purple rain drops
through our fingertips and seeps brown into the sand
We were two diamonds stranded on a deserted island
Useless, like earmuffs in Southern California.

sore foot

ain't nothin right nowadays
always seem like nuthin change
like a big fat pimp
walkin with a limp
is it cuz he cucumber cool
legs so long ya kin tell he ain't no fool
comin down off ta tallahachee mountain
but he been workin' these streets for years
could it jes be that he tard?
An' the limp really come from a sore foot?
...
Got a black dog with fur all over his face
He looks at me with a man's eyes
I takes him ever'whar an' he follers
Jes cool as kin be
Laps at the motel pool wit the leabs still in it
Gets a quick drank and moseys on
After whall he gits tard too
And the bur in his web toe gets wedged in good
And he's walkin with the limp but do he care?
I dunno, won't let me tech it,
must do like it, I guess
...
Down at the bus stop
Under a hot august sun, a young gal and her daughter
Set down on a broken down seat with graffiti telephone numbers on it
Young gal fans haself and then the little girl
The little girl asts to walk a spell
Mama say stay near, takin' off her heel and rubbin her sore bunion.
Little girl peeks out and the hot sun beats her but she thinks least there's a
breeze
She walks a few steps, looks back into mama's watchful eye
Walks a few more steps
The sun is blinding, man its hot
And ain't no breeze after all
Walks a-ways, she feels like the earth is slipping from beneath her
leg held high like she hurt it, little girl tips over slow and faints dead away
Onto the hot pavement stained with bubble gum as pink's her shirt

It say "Cute and Cuddly Kitten" wit a pitcher of a little cat on it.
Cute.
Mama don't see her at first and looks around, then sees the crowd gatherin
down the street a-ways.
She run, gets there in a flash,
Holdin' her baby near, she pats those flushed and heated cheeks
Her lips pale against the hot-house tomato color flushing her brown cheeks
Mama says "speak to me, where are we?, what's your name?…" like so.
Somebody asts if they can help.
Mama don't hear. Ears all plugged up with frettin'. But after a while, it's
safe to chuckle, little girl plays with her doll at her mother's side. Folks can
see, by the way she ran over, her foot sho ain't sore. Nope, not no mo.

hard case

pap is a wife beater
his son's a poet
every day he beats his wife
is another poem lost
boy's soul a-curlin' up inside him
and the beatins just keep comin'
screamin and a-yellin
screechin and a-hollerin

...

woman's got no dignity
with her hair snatched out
man's just an ogre
but ain't no fiction to him
just a fist and a cuss
and a empty 40 ounce

...

This is home to a boy
with poems in his heart
but his soul's so curled up that the heart turns blue
and he can't seem to breathe
and his time runs out

...

his girlfriend got a black eye
just like his mama
and he don't write no more

...

It's all a shame
what can you do
but place the blame
where do it go
go very slow
back to the beginning of time
where the first poet had his rhyme
but some devil had to add his dumb 2 cent
and now its all discordant

Mist in the Valley

A thin mist hovers above the mountains
Gravity introduces light droplets to green hills
Sun illuminates gray clouds, turns them brighter
Birds chirp quietly
No brazen crow's call is heard
The valley is quiet

…

Crisp, dead ground turns fresh, growing new and green before our eyes
Trees shoot new limbs up, out of old ones,
Emboldened by a slaked thirst and a gentle, consistent sun
Disappearing one day, reappearing the next,
The sun rests elsewhere from time to time
And the valley writes thank you notes in orange, yellow and purple
When the sun stays away long enough, the valley becomes selective
Always welcoming rain, enjoying light occasional meals out with sun

…

The hills awaken slowly
Like a pubescent child
Quiet, lazy, until they burst forth with emotion at the slightest jarring
Pine tree fronds shoot forth and curve upward
As if cupping precious sustenance which drops, radiant, out of thin air

…

Selective tree limbs, lacking eyes and ears, reach deaf and blind toward a
flower-shunned sun
Unable to walk, those trees reach outward, desiring what the valley rejected
Those trees that have, will gain
Those have not, will lose
Or reach
And find, like the rest

…

Sun and rain descend together,
the sweet rarity of their meeting prompting glares of envy
from romantic rain's lover moon.
Vultures cease hovering.
Gentle drops from the sky have wet the tongue of the tired doe in the forest
She regains her footing
Tiptoeing, enlivened by the wet on her cheeks, on her tongue
She finds her calf who calls her from a distance.

They move on.

…

Even to them, it is a wide world; especially so.
Lovely in its horror
To its own self, true, and to no other.
The snake strikes the mouse.
The salamander slithers under a log, just out of reach of the raccoon's sharp claw.
Still, a thin mist hovers above the mountains.
All is quiet in the valley.

Hungry sweet bread

The new school teacher at the Indian School gets off the bus and stands before the one room schoolhouse sitting tidily at the top of the hill. Dense, dark mountains loom all around her. Though she feels small, she takes a look around and feels a bit more at ease.

A little brown-skinned girl comes down the walk and greets her.

"What's your name, little girl?"

"Rosita," the girl answers. She smiles the smile of a bright flower not yet bloomed in the fresh dew of the morning. Rosita's face was like a flower that awaits the sun patiently, knowing it will come because it has never known a day without the sun.

"Rosita, where are your shoes?" the teacher asks, inquisitively.

"I have none," answers Rosita.

"You have no shoes?" asks the teacher again, her brow furrowing slightly as the sun creeps up over the eastern ridge of mountains. "Where do you live?"

The little brown-skinned girl took the new teacher's hand and led her up the stony path. Turning into one of the small houses, the little girl led the teacher inside.

"Come in," Rosita says, smiling.

"Rosita, you have no door," says the teacher, her eyes wide.

"I know," says Rosita and she led the teacher inside. "I'd only have to open it, if I did."

The new school teacher at the Indian School stands inside, looking all around in dismay.

"Rosita…Rosita…you have no refrigerator…"

"I know," says Rosita. "The garden is outside the door. I pick and eat anytime I'm hungry." Rosita smiles and shows the new teacher a handful of tomatoes fresh off the vine. "And when Mama makes bread, she borrows honey from the bees and bakes bread in the sun." Rosita licks her lips. "It's so sweet I'm not hungry for the whole day."

"No running water," continues the new teacher as she walks about, not listening to Rosita.

"I know," smiles Rosita. "The river runs all the time, right over there," Rosita points to the running river just behind the garden.

The new school teacher looks at the little brown-skinned girl in alarm, hesitating just a moment. "…so poor…"

"I know," says Rosita, smiling as the sun beams out brilliantly from behind a cloud. Rosita's smile is in full bloom. "I'm poor!" she says happily, thinking it's a complement.

And for many years afterward, Rosita tells all her friends, "I'm poor!!" and proudly sings and dances, eating many of her mother's honey cakes in her garden by the river.

the earth QUAKES

the earth quakes over itchy fault lines that shift as if asleep and dreaming
their own rumbling wakes them up, makes them toss and turn as the ages
pass.
we are tossed and turned in our beds while the rumbling turns to rapid
jolting which terrifies our dogs and sets our pictures askew on the wall

…

we sleep fitfully afterward, remembering how irritable I was just before the
rumbling started. I, like an animal in the wild with nerves set on edge,
felt the press of two terrestrial edges which, miles in length, scratched and
twanged against each other in a run for peace in Earth

…

all seems peaceful. All seems right, but the earth knows things we know
not, knows the outcome of rumors and wars. The earth has seen it all,
having borne the footfalls of all who've ever walked. The dogged trail of
humanity is etched deeply into sagging folds of earth, rivers and sky.

…

In fact, the earth quakes beneath roadside bombs strewn across dusty
bridges and
It trembles beneath gale-force winds authored by man-made climate change.
Like knobby-kneed old men playing bocce ball on manicured lawns where
once they played stick ball on the block, the Earth struggles to renew itself
even whilst its agedness is unmistakable. It is seen, perfectly perceptible,
and known acutely by all living and dead.

…

Undoubtedly, the earth is an entity; if not a mother, then certainly a child.
As an innocent victim, a survivor, it quakes in fear and pain like the rest of
us.

…

Like a precocious child who knows both joyful expectation of spring and
the painful lash of landmines, the earth quakes with the peaks and valleys
of erudition. Yet, despite the temptation toward the vanity of supposed
supreme knowledge, the earth is humbled by a mere look. It, like all else,
trembles before its Master. Lightning flashes and those who walk the earth
cower and stand up only to marvel.

…

The earth stands and becomes active when, occur, the three things that
shouldn't: The earth will not stand still. It shifts to restore what is right.

Its trembling sends a destroying paroxysm along earthly channels straight to the heart of the wrong borne along on it.

…

Under the anger of the Almighty, the earth trembles. The nations tremble and pass away, forgotten, swallowed up in wrath.

…

The earth stands and moves, wobbles and unfolds. At a word, the mountain moves into the sea. The earth quakes at the footfalls of its Master.

Things That Make You Go Hmm...

The flight of bees and airplanes
The inner workings of automobiles and the human brain
The instant contagion of yawns
Advanced engineering styles of ancient cultures
The way of wives with their husbands and children
The beauty of thriving horticulture
The intensity of an infant's gaze
The evolution of dance
Why dead cells slough off
The benefits of community to living things
The existence of mosquitoes
The relationship of growth & decay
The color variations of a rainbow
The perfection and beauty of sleeping children
Nanotechnology and gray goo
The difference between opinion and truth
The joys of a clean slate
Why sweet tastes better than bitter
The adornment of young women, flowers and peacocks
Everything under (and over) the sun...

Will the revolution be televised?

Will the revolution be televised?
Commercialism evacuating the sudsy vacuums of our minds
I ask should the fists be raised or the guns drawn?
Or shall we use both to raze these lines of silent demarcation
Tramp on the rectangular manicured lawns,
Pull up the sprinklers by their plastic roots and track angry, loud and
conspicuous mud on the 3-inch thick pile carpet on which 400-year-old
spirits float, tip-toeing careful and obedient even in the afterlife.
Afraid of death even when we are immersed in it.
The slow and romantic on-screen deaths belie the pop pop pop of the steel
in the streets.
I ask, when will we set our sights on the Hills and the Valley beyond?
When will we burn, trash and loot the not-so-productive but still efficient
colonies of our own psychology?
Will the Twinkie-mouthed interviewer still mince loaded guns with
assumptions of meaninglessness and parade lies in front of the camera while
we watch with elephants' eyes?
...

Will he blink camera-ready eyes oozing with concern, showing carefully
capped teeth and the reconstructed mouth of those who practice their
smiles in front of mirrors?
Will we watch and believe?
Will he deign to air 30 minutes of encapsulated chaos as we air the
centuries-encrusted laundry dampened by our soul-tears for generations?
Will there be enough juice for the camera to roll, run and play?
Will our screens only flicker or will the story just make us sicker?
Will they still love this land when it all of it hits the fan?
Info blurbs and catch-phrases still linger from 60's past.
Will our struggle be satisfied with glorious justice and a level playing field or
quenched with idealisms made more "practical" by a dollar bill?
Stop tape on that.
That news is not for the delicate palate.
Better wait til after the 11 o'clock.

...

Will we be fed last years reruns when the smell of smoke permeates the fabric of our insulated lives?

Will we watch?

Will we beg for the newest and latest "reality", even as our sons and daughters enlist?

The fire creeping up our lawns with the insistence of a scorned lover back for what's his.

Will we sit glued to the tube, in denial and denied as we ever were, shotgun across our laps, giving pause to no reason, grateful for Tivo.

Just the sound of cans falling off the shelf.

Will it be like Orson Wells's alien broadcast?

Or Fox selling like they never sold before?

…

Will the revolution be televised?

Like the filmic yogurt of obsession and alien-possession, will we buy it with the fury of emotionally-deprived, spiritually obese children with chocolate-cake in hand?

Will we fry it and serve it with our vegetables, molding new realities like tofu, let it absorb all the old flavors of a trusted friend's politics until it's digestible, if just a little gamey?

in his wake

they brought him in wearing a black tuxedo
I could not tell if he wore tails
As he lay on them and would not move
As hard as I glared at him, he did not flutter an eyelash
I wailed and cried with all my might and he did not budge
So unlike him.
…
When they took me
back to my seat and wrapped me in my shawl
It began to dawn on me that you were not coming back
When they cried before me and patted my hand afterward
I wanted to eat some of the food (it looked so delicious) and chat
I looked for you to tell that joke you tell so well
But you were not there
…
They left you in that box – smaller than I thought it would be
Though you did not look cramped
I left my kerchief on your chest
I know how you like the smell of my neck
But I have a feeling that smell will stay where it is
Instead of waft into your waiting nostrils
Those precious nostrils are under ground
And will smell no more.

The City Rushes

The city rushes like an ocean against my ears in the rain.
I watch traffic lights spin green stars from my eyes off of a thousand
buildings.
Twinkling slow as if under water.
Limousines swift as eels through the muck.
Bloody darkness, yellow lights splashing against cabs racing
blue steel, badges, policemen, sharks, slow-weaving and ready.
…

Pelted softly, steadily by insistent drops.
I'm deferred by insistent wheels against puddles.
Turning wheels against puddles of transparent blackness.
Awash with sleepy girls holding champagne glasses aloft
In a centuries-old pose of gaiety.
Summed up in high heels and lipstick, their cabs arrive as
Aimless swimmers against the strong, dark current of nightlife.
…

New York is a mess of soot.
An ocean of fish drowning in air.
Slipping here and there…Back and forth…in front of my eyes reflecting
green and yellow and red.
The horns and laughter careen loud against my silent ocean sensibilities.
I yearn madly, unfooled by the steady beat of my heart, for the moon to tug
me.
Pulling me up and pushing me down, bring me forth and send me back.
To pull at my depths and make them leap and break, crushing down upon
sleeping minds and searching hearts.
…

Sweeping over dark rushes of night.
Quietly, quietly, halting the wheels.
Chasing the eels, crushing them like snakes under heel.
Sweeping, sweeping in and over the dim blue lights.
The stars and moon.
My heart pulling me after it, dragging body after soul until there are no
more waves to break
Or ears to hurt
Deafened by the sound, the insistent sound , the splash of wheels on
dirty pavement in a sea of wealth like the sharks and whales that rule the
underbelly of the city.

I compare you to a night's sky

Crickets' song fills the air
Mingling with toads' rhythmic calls
Sounds of dirt under wheels of an old pick-up
Then silence

Giant trees all around
Water gurgling in deep pools after rain
I sit next to you as you read a book in an upper room
Looking up at me, you are silent

You rub Vick's Vaporub, doing battle with my congestion
I cough pathetically in thanks
You forgive my wheezing as I sleep
As the stars gleam brightly overhead

Deepest night covers us
The quietude of the natural world
The sky comforts me like a blanket –
consistent and immense like the arms of a husband

Singing with the crickets,
I puff my chest out in pride like the toad by water's edge
We peel out, jubilant, in your '57 Chevy
I go quiet in the seat beside you

The night sky holds me like you do.
Constant and immense.
My face stands out in the light shining through your moonroof
You illuminate me under the rich, deep, radiant cover of your arms.

A Child's Poem

Sunlight is beautiful.
When I sit on my bed and dream,
the sunlight peeks through the window and
I come and say, "play with me",
But it goes away.
I laugh and just say, "the sunlight is shy. It will come again."

Alive

Sign your name on the dotted line
The responsibility lies in your hands
And on your will to live

They will be tested.
One to the bone, the other may perhaps be broken.
Like the promise of America.
You work, you eat, you pay, you go, you do, you drive, you try, and breathe.
Don't forget that one.
'Else Pete is a goner and so too your father's dreams.

Stress is the mother of all calamities.
It brings pain
And leaves nothing to be counted,
Only that which to chalk up as a loss…
Time is its fuel.

Forebearance is widowed at the bullfight and market of distress
If they've got something to buy,
You'll sell it all…
The peace of mind you hoped to inherit with your wits,
the sanity to which you were born
You know it can be put off no longer.
Commit to the dance of death or die.
You're alive, but barely.

You have neither time nor energy to debate the issue.
Not to mention patience.
You've lost it all.
Recovery snickers behind your back, don't you hear?
Its idol, hope, and crony, one-step-at-a-time, laugh too, just out of reach.

You don't know whether to turn and spit or just ignore them
They get on your nerves. Just the idea of them makes you darn mad.
Recovery, hope and patience:
Sweetness and light on the outside,
Innocent and accessible as stray puppies on a local street corner.

You begin to believe they're really just the popular girls you always loved to hate.
More like envied.
You don't remember their names, but oh!
Their faces, their boyfriends, taunt and flaunt perfect hair and teeth
Perfect houses and perfect Saturday nights at you from past decades.

They're probably fat and divorced now.
You try not to laugh.
But, why not laugh?

That perfect hair was really just a mullet.
If that's so, then maybe hope really is true and exceptionally funny
because of its unpredictability and its colossal sense of humor.

One day death and next day a sunrise.
Isn't that the way of it?
Isn't it true and so funny how we hold that towel at the edge of the ring
And stop, mid-throw,
because hope says 'Wait just a minute, I've got something for you.'

Patience starts talking, talking slow as always, but talking
Telling you to put down the right and then the left and so on.
And you do it too because hope promised, remember?

And recovery catches up with you, breathless as you are from all that walking
More like jogging and you're no tri-athlete
But recovery starts singing a song
And it's not a dirge.
More like ragtime than the blues

And you hum the tune while you march
Because it's your salvation
And you're alive, but you dare not believe it.

Pretty soon, you greet the day like it's relish on a hot dog
You may not like relish, but with ketchup and mustard and everything else,
relish blends right in and even leaves a pleasant aftertaste.

And like that, you kiss your husband and actually feel his lips.

The onions on his breath don't repel you.
You smile.
You pet your dog and you know she's yours and the cutest one
And she was FREE and, though she won't last forever, she really is a darn
good dog.

You're your husband's lover.
And if asked who loves you, all the time, rain or shine,
you'd have to say both the dog and him.

Somehow, the bills get paid,
the food eaten, and hurts are felt then forgotten.
And though your steps sometimes falter, they keep coming.

And you're alive…
And you're alive…
And you're alive…

Christmas is Everyday

They say that Christmastime is but once a year
A holiday of warmth in winter
When peoples celebrate, drinking in good cheer
and goodness in the hearts of most where nothing bad can splinter

but I say let there be Christmas everyday
that men and ladies may be merry
and walk together and with God in the sweetest way
that burdens of our brethren all, may be cheerfully carried

Though our days are short and like a breath,
My wish is light may dispel the night and light the pathways narrow
That peace and hope and blessedness will shut the eager jaws of death
And remember love for one and all 'cause His eye is on the sparrow

Yes, Christmas! Christmas! Everyday!
That joy in life abound
And children, aging, will nary say
God cursed this cold, hard ground

But only, laughing, for joy untold
Enjoying every good thing under the sun
Striding across the globe, lions free and bold
Wishing health and prosperity, yes, God Bless Us, Every One!

I could and I think I might

I could quit tomorrow and no-one could stop me
I could lay it all on the line and no-one could reprieve me
I don't need the money
Nope, don't need the money at all
I been poor before and it ain't so bad
Got the Lord, don't I?
Don't need no garbage.
My today's got enough garbage of it's own without yours from yesterday
Don't see no landfills here, do ya?
I could and I think I might
Get outta here and never come back

But I won't
Cuz I likes it here and I mean to stay
Nothing you can do unless God say so
And He ain't said nothin' to me bout it.
So we'll just have to see
But til then, don't give me no bother and I'll keep my bother tethered on a
strong leash
So don't be feared and I won't either. An' g'night.

I love you this much

Because you protect me from the storms of doubt that rage and freeze my
bones
I love you as much as I love a warm hat on a cold winter day
Because you comfort me and wrap me in your soft loving arms
I love you as much as I love my favorite pair of blue jeans
Because you lift me up and keep me floating several feet off the floor
I love you as much as I love the bed we share
Because you make me feel welcome and like where you are is home
I love you as much as I love our house that we bought together, you and I
Because you are sweet and satisfying and leave me wanting more
I love you as much as I love the last chocolate truffle
Because you make me laugh and tickle me pink though I am brown
I love you as much as I love a late-night Abbott and Costello movie
Because you always smell good with no perfume necessary
I love you as much as I love the smell of pine trees in the forest of our yard
As much as I love the aroma of baking oatmeal raisin cookies
As much as I adore the scent of your face just behind your ear
As much as I crave a whiff of anything you're cooking
Day and night, for all twelve months and trebled on a leap year,
I love you this much, my dear.

i wear the garb of combat

i wear the garb of combat
the fatigue green jacket in the style of a soldier
I wear it because I am one
I deny myself as a soldier does
I do not engage in gossip, slander, malicious talk.
I do not curse or lie.

My life is not taken up with the strategies of self profit
My life's work is to bring glory to His Majesty, the King
I work for the Almighty
I am one of the enlisted ones
I consider it my everyday task, one of my highest duties, in fact,
to bring peace to the region in which I am stationed.

I bring news of the deepest peace, the most significant peace…inner peace.
This is not the propaganda most governors feed their constituents
It is true and real.
This peace occurs within one's heart.
As a soldier in the service of the Prince of Peace, my highest duty is to love.
In my civilian life, I work as a farmer.
I sew seeds of peace, of love and grace.
And I don my soldier's garb interchangeably with these well-worn
dungarees.

I am a soldier, foremost.
The peace I bring is not the sort forced upon unwilling captives.
If the peace I bring were to permeate the world entirely, there would be no
war, no conflict unsolved, no strife un-squelched.
I fight selfishness and discord, I battle hatred and oppression, I counsel
greed and envy until it is no more, I forgive despite wounds, I minister
reconciliation. My mission is to reach out, though some days my hands sift
through emptiness. I turn my cheek, I pray for the enemy. I love and more;
The peace I bring is love.
I am a soldier of the Almighty God.

Passive aggression

Yes, this is going to be a rant
so don't blame me if you feel like crap afterward
I told you ahead of time, so let's hurry and get it over with

Don't ya hate it when somebody smiles, and inside you know they're
sneering at you?
Don't ya hate it when someone compliments your skirt, and inside they're
assessing your paycheck to see if it's designer or not? And then they smile
cuz they know it must be a knockoff.
Don't you hate it when someone tells you they know what you mean or,
worse, know how you feel when they really don't and, on top of that, don't
care either?
Don't you hate it when someone thinks that they know what is best, but
you know that the best they're thinking of is really just the kind of "best"
that applies to their very own selves and that's all.
Don't you hate it when someone says they'll help, and then they don't? say
they care and then they won't? say they can, and then say they can't when,
really, they can?
Don't ya hate that?
Don't ya just hate it?
…Yeah.

Plans

Plan B is for fools without a decent Plan A...
Some say

But something tells you when Plan A is alright, but alright just isn't good
enough, one must make...
Plan B

Because what if, one day, you wake up and find out that Plan A is for
suckers who shelved their sense of adventure sometime after college in favor
of a decent paycheck. And, gasp, what if the paycheck is better with...
Plan B

What if, what if, says the idle, fearful mind. Then Plan A.
Maybe so, maybe so, the grudging admission of a bored mind...but Plan B.

Warring plans fire missiles that haunt your dreams, making fodder for
nightmares.
Waking up in a sweat, you wonder, what if and maybe there is, hidden
among the lukewarm coals keeping your heart chugging along, a jewel, a
diamond, something new... what if and maybe there is just, simply, only,
really, finally a...
Plan Be
Choosing one or the other, in the end there is just Be, only Be, finally Be.
So you relax and Be

Or make Plan C and learn how to do that.

sea washed tree

stormy winds whistle through the darkened land
in the pure darkness, fragrant with evergreen
the roots of a five hundred year old colossus
give, having clung to land for too long,
uprooted, washing downstream
finding the ocean
rolling, rolling through muddy gullies
limbs torn and branches lanced
lashed against rock and scraped against smooth stone laying at rushing river
bottom
leafless tree, stripped
washed clean in salt and fresh water, alternately
lay twisted in sand
yes, torn from the forest
gray, smooth, naked
beautiful,
adorned by nothing but land and sea

Suzie's Boy

Suzie had a baby boy,
His name was Bobby. Bob, in a few years.
Well, Bob was a kite-flyer.
A regular at the park across the way
And he begged his Mama daily to let him go.

She said no.
So Bob decided one day he'd go,
He'd go for good.
Scraped those dollars from his family's trust, and left.
Took that trust with him.

He found a town and that town found him
And he found a pub. A hole, more like.
And boy did Bob dance. Girl upon girl, drink, dance.
Danced all night.
Danced so long Bobby got tired, but the dance wasn't over.
Wasn't near over.
Not til he said so.

That boy, Suzie's Bobby, had big ol' ears, I remember.
His Mama'd loved those ears, Papa's ears
She's say and smile.

And Bob tried to forget.
Takes a while to forget stuff like that. So he gave it a while.
One day, while he was waiting.
He began to feel like a pig…
The way he wanted everything, bought everything, drank everything, threw
everything away, but still, still there was that SUN   that wouldn't go away.

I recall, Papa couldn't believe his eyes.
He cried, even. Took him in his arms and forgot the past.
My son is back, at last.

The other son wasn't quick to accept
Mad at the traitor who was back on their step.
After all, he'd worked double-hard for free, hadn't he?

And he set his arms and his ways, and refused.

And Papa said "Boy, I love you. Everything I have is yours.
You stood by me when lion reared and the furnace was cold.
Wasn't nothing bringing him but love.
You gotta put pain behind your back
And be grateful when the rope is slack
Or none of us would have a chance.
You gotta look forward to a new day.

But, try as he might, he'd fight that light.
Fight the memory of the kite.
Bite the sight of night in flight.
One day, he'd see, like from a great height…
Bobby was a brother,
His slate, clean and white.
Right….alright…

When he saw, he'd seen what a sight Bobby was.
Longing for that food, it left him hungry.
And ashamed.
"Stinking land of stingy people.
And I'm a fool", Bob'd say, when he curled up on the hay.
Seemed like his bones ached.

Then, one day, Bob woke up.
Put an end to the deadness of his mind.
He woke up in the sun's bright rays.
Said he came to his senses, in the light of day.
Said he'd find his way.

Vowed to be a better man, not a stranger's hired hand.
I've done what is wrong.
I'm here to do right.
Take me, I'm a servant, Papa.
Forgive me this night.

He saw the place in the distance.
There across the hills, a lone man stood.
Bobby saw a figure coming close.
Could see he was running.

And Suzie said through her tears...
Bobby's still got his big ole ears
Don't ya know I love those ears.
Got Papa's ears, to this day.

Smile, Bobby, Papa loves you.
Better than if you'd never went away.

The Painter

Exotic birds delicately adorned
Rotated in palm of painter's hand
Living rainbows set across naked wings,
Dried by celestial breezes
Set aloft by glory
Caught by terrestrial wind
Vanished amid miles of blue, blue sky and waves of deeper blue
Going on past horizons as far as the eye can see

Toes in the Heather

Toes in the heather are mine and yours
Bundle of joy held between us
We play footsie and remember how this baby was made
Balmy sun browns our aging skin
Baby soft skin is a marvel, something we have made
Tiny toes in the heather

unmasking

I thought I was free when I did the forbidden things
Hidden things too hideous to do in the open
I reveled in the shattering of taboo though at times it coincided with my
conscience
It was overlooked

I cravenly sought the things that said freedom but brought slavery
I was beholden to those who held the key to all those mysterious and
universal locks
When they said go, I went
When they said stop, I halted, stomach in my throat, awaiting their next
command

Then I saw myself in the mirror and I looked away, shocked.
Looking again, I could not look away until that face was put aright.
I peeled the layers, the caked on makeup that just wasn't my color
The fake nose and tinted iris of haughty-eyed party girl popular with all
except myself

I shook out my hair, this was still much unchanged, not much you can do
with it
Thank God for tomorrow. The perm grows out by millimeters with each
passing moment.

I look in the mirror once more and I see smudges.
I besmirched the mask but it still held fast though in pieces
In need of a wash, I was baptized in the streams of humility
To Christ I came and he broke me free
Melting makeup left my face with a shriek. I did not know makeup could
do that.

I left my mask in the tub,
The dirty Harlem tub on the 3rd floor on the East side of a life heading due
West

My city streets have turned to country lanes
When I alight from the coach, I wear nothing more than sunscreen
when I walk, I do not stoop

but glide on a confidence new-found

I will not let the worst take hold of me
I will shake the dust from my destiny
I will triumph over sin and slavery

Working man

Elbows leaned against an old wood table
Propped over a steaming plate of the evening's best
Shoveling mouthfuls of the stuff down an eager gullet
Appreciative grunts and smiles ascend from a southward bending face
He eats like he works
All quick clean motions and laser focus
A git 'r done attitude sucks up the last drop
Eyes glazed over, a ceasing of work
A long grateful belch
Patting the belly

...

On goes the tv, clicker in hand
It's football season and his favorite team is doing well
Settles down into a well-worn couch,
his form snuggling, familiar, into the dip in the middle
wraps a dusty arm round the cook's neck
settles in for the evening
today's, yes even tomorrow's hard row forgotten for a few quiet hours

...

"sleep is sweet for the laborer"[1]
Morning sun enters slowly, steadily over the thin coverlet
Peeling back the layers of man's dreams:
Golf expeditions and lunar landings, safaris and a miraculous cure for
increasing debt
The man awakes, there is no dawdling
A yawn and a hot shower precede a hot cup o' joe
A kiss from the missus
And off he goes

...

Day after day, year after year
Eggs are bought, and if they're paying overtime, bacon too
So go the years, decades roll like silent avalanches
Working man's work is done not with the coming of gray hair
But only when the light in the eyes in dimmed too deeply
And the fingers won't grasp the hammer or chisel or saw or stake
Then, only then, is his work truly done

...

---

1   Book of Proverbs, The Bible

He can lay his gray head down one last time after sup
and a hug from the missus seals it with love.
And heaven is where he can still taste her cooking
and she's there, or will be soon
And when she is, her apron is off
and that moon shot is only a step away.

About the Author

From a young age, her love of truth and its poetic expression on the written page compelled Nuñez to read voraciously and to write her thoughts as close to her inmost core as possible, keeping an impeccable record of them through the years.

It was by means of her education in various forms of writing by playwright Ari Roth at the University of Michigan, writer/filmmakers Sandra Berg and Todd Boyd at the University of Southern California, and writer Steve Hellman at Mendocino College, that Nuñez developed her unique style of poetic storytelling.

Steeping herself in the lore of the Good Book, travelling the world for inspiration, sampling and giving the treasures of literary humanity: the spoken and written word, Nuñez builds up literary steam the further she journeys along her inimitable path.

Influenced by poetic greats such as Ginsburg, Poe, Tennyson, Hughes, Angelou, and McKay, Nuñez infuses her work with tones of deep respect for those trailblazers as well as with a playful irreverence for traditional forms of poetic language.

After years of prompting by her father, mother and husband, Nuñez decided to throw her hat into the ring as a writer and poet. *Things that Make You Go Hmm ... A poetic tour of introspection and other curiosities* is her first collection of poems to gain public release.

Nuñez lives in the Pacific coastal forest of Northern California with her husband and child. Her works of fiction, photography and children's stories are set for release in the coming months. We have no doubt that you will enjoy this and those with much gusto.